He Fought for Freedom
FREDERICK DOUGLASS

by Virginia Schomp

Based on the Writings of Frederick Douglass

BENCHMARK BOOKS

MARSHALL CAVENDISH
NEW YORK

All the quotes in this book are from Frederick Douglass's three autobiographies: *Narrative of the Life of Frederick Douglass, an American Slave; My Bondage and My Freedom;* and *Life and Times of Frederick Douglass.*

Benchmark Books
Marshall Cavendish Corporation
99 White Plains Road
Tarrytown, New York 10591-9001

Library of Congress Cataloging-in-Publication Data
Schomp, Virginia, date
Frederick Douglass : He Fought for Freedom / by Virginia Schomp.
p.   cm. — (Benchmark biographies)
Includes bibliographical references and index.
Summary: Relates the life story of the former slave and famous abolitionist.
!SBN 0-7614-0488-0 (lib. bdg.)
1. Douglass, Frederick, 1817?–1895—Juvenile literature. 2. Afro-American abolitionists—Biography—Juvenile literature.
3. Abolitionists—United States—Biography—Juvenile literature. 4. Slaves—United States—Biography—Juvenile literature.
[1. Douglass, Frederick, 1817?–1895. 2. Abolitionists. 3. Afro-Americans—Bijography.] I. Title. II. Series.
E449.D75S36   1997   973.7'114'092—dc20   96-2401   CIP   AC

Printed in Hong Kong

Photo research by Virginia Schomp and Richard Bigness

Photo Credits. Front cover: courtesy of © North Wind Picture Archives; back cover: courtesy of National Portrait Gallery, Smithsonian Institution; pages 4, 28(center), 29: Anacostia Museum; pages 6, 9, 11, 18, 20, 24(top), 24(bottom), 36, 39, 43: © North Wind Picture Archives; page 10: Boston Athenaeum; pages 13, 16, 26, 31: The Bettman Archive; pages 19, 28(left), 28(right); Moorland-Spingarn Research Center, Howard University; page 23: Old Dartmouth Historical Society—New Bedford Whaling Museum; page 27: UPI/Bettmann; page 33: The Metropolitan Museum of Art, Gift of Mr. and Mrs. Carl Stoeckel, 1897; page 34: The Lincoln Museum, Fort Wayne, IN; pages 40, 41: National Park Service, Frederick Douglass National Historic Site.

1   3   5   6   4   2

To Richard,
for endless patience, help, and encouragement

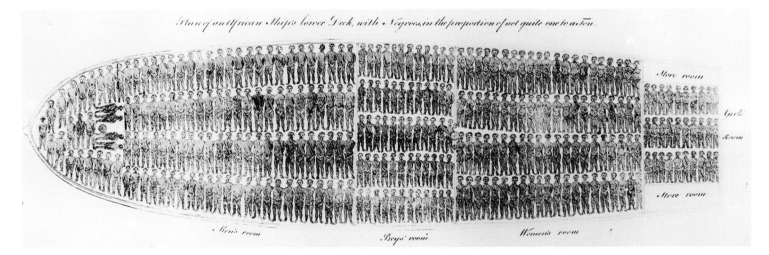

In the days of slavery, many black men, women, and children made the long journey from Africa in hot, crowded slave ships.

CONTENTS

Slaves were sold at auctions to whoever agreed to pay the highest price.

BORN A SLAVE

Loud voices woke Frederick. He peeked through a crack in the door. His pretty Aunt Hester was standing on a stool, with her hands tied to a hook in the kitchen ceiling. Behind her stood Old Master. He held a whip. Twenty, thirty, forty times the man beat Hesther's bleeding back, while she cried in pain. Frederick watched, shaking. If he tried to help, it might be his turn next.

"I had never seen any thing like it before," Frederick later wrote. The seven-year-old had only been with Old Master a short time. Before that, he had lived in a cabin in the woods with his Grandmamma Betsy. The cabin was small and poor, but to Frederick it was a cozy, loving home. Then, one day, his grandmother had taken his hand and walked him twelve long miles to Old Master's farm. There she left him. He never saw her again. That was when the boy began to understand what it meant to be a slave.

LIFE ON THE PLANTATION

Slavery was an old part of American life by 1824, the year Frederick went to live with Old Master. For more than two hundred years, white slave traders had sailed to Africa and bought or captured black men, women, and children. They brought their prisoners to America and sold them like animals, to work for a master for life. Most slaves worked on plantations, or large farms, in the South. Slavery was a cheap way for plantation owners to get the work done in their homes and fields.

Aaron Anthony—the man called Old Master—was manager of the largest plantation on the Eastern Shore of Maryland, where Frederick was born. Anthony owned Frederick's grandmother and his mother, Harriet Bailey.

Frederick only saw his mother four or five times. She was sent to work on a neighbor's farm and died when he was very young. He never even knew who his father was. People said he had a white father, but even if that was true, it didn't matter. Any child of a slave mother was a slave himself, born belonging to her master.

Aaron Anthony was a cruel master. He gave his slaves just enough food to stay alive and working. The children ate corn-meal mush from a feeding tray on the floor. Frederick was always hungry. He was often cold, too. Children had only two long shirts a year—no pants or jackets, socks or shoes. They had no beds or blankets. Frederick slept in an empty corn sack on the floor of a closet by the kitchen.

Plantation owners lived in fine houses, dressed in fine clothes, and ate from tables piled high with food.

Plantation slaves lived in tiny, run-down shacks.

From then on, the boy couldn't stop thinking about slavery. What gave slave owners their power? Why did the masters dress in fine clothes and eat good food, while the slaves, who did all the work, went cold and hungry? Years later, Frederick wrote that these questions filled him with "a burning hatred of slavery." By the time he was eight years old, he had made up his mind that he would be free someday.

CITY BOY

Frederick could hardly believe his luck. After two years on the plantation, he was going on an adventure. Old Master's daughter Lucretia was sending him to Baltimore, to work for her husband's family.

Baltimore! Frederick had heard exciting stories about that big, busy city. As

That's where he was the morning he saw Old Master whip Aunt Hesther.

In the early 1800s, ships loaded with goods from all over the world passed through Baltimore's harbor.

he stood on the tall ship sailing into Baltimore harbor, he was amazed by the jumble of buildings and people. Even more wonderful was the kind, smiling face of his new mistress.

Sophia Auld had never had a slave before. She treated Frederick like any other child. The boy ate at the family table. He slept in his own warm bed. His only chores were running errands for Sophia and keeping an eye on her two-year-old son, Tommy. When Tommy climbed into his mother's lap to hear a storybook, Frederick felt almost like another son standing by her side.

Reading was a mystery to Frederick. How did those black marks on the page become words? When he asked Sophia to teach him, she gladly agreed. In no time, Frederick learned the alphabet.

Then Sophia's husband, Hugh, found out about the lessons.

Teaching a slave to read was against the law, Hugh shouted. Angrily he warned his wife that the more Frederick learned, the harder it would be to keep him a slave.

That ended Sophia's reading lessons. But Frederick knew his most important lesson had come from Hugh Auld. *Learning* was the secret behind the slave owner's power. Learning would help make him free.

SECRET STUDENT

It took Frederick seven years to teach himself to read and write. Sometimes he talked young white friends into showing him what they learned in school. One boy gave him an old spelling book, and

As a young boy, Frederick Douglass learned about the abolitionists— a group of people who were working to end slavery. Years later, he gave a fiery speech at an abolitionist meeting like this one, and became one of the group's most famous leaders.

Frederick studied it till he knew every word by heart. When the Aulds went out, he copied Tommy's school lessons or sneaked a peek at books and, newspapers.

By the time he was twelve, Frederick

had saved up enough pennies to buy his own book, *The Columbian Orator*. The book was filled with speeches by famous men. Frederick's favorite speech was about the unfairness of slavery. He read it aloud to himself many times, practicing the new, fine-sounding words.

In newspapers, Frederick learned another powerful new word—*abolition*. He knew that somewhere up North were Free States, where slavery was no longer allowed. Now he learned that some people were trying to end, or abolish, slavery down south, too. Some of these abolitionists even helped slaves run away to the Free States.

Reading about the work of people who hated slavery gave Frederick hope. The time was coming for his own run for freedom.

FROM SLAVERY TO FREEDOM

While Frederick was in Baltimore, Old Master and his daughter Lucretia died. Lucretia's husband, Thomas Auld, became the boy's new owner. In 1833, Thomas ordered his slave home.

Frederick was fifteen now, tall, strong, and proud. He would not bow his head and call Thomas Auld "master." Instead of jumping to follow orders, he was slow. He pretended not to understand. Auld complained that city life had spoiled Frederick.

Maybe the slave breaker Edward Covey could help. The way some people broke wild horses, taming them so they would work for a master, Covey broke hard-to-manage slaves. Frederick was sent to Covey's farm. For six months, he worked in the slave breaker's fields. From before sunup till late at night, in snow and rain, cold and burning heat, he worked. No matter how hard he worked, Covey whipped him. Soon his body felt crushed and his mind filled with darkness.

Slaves worked in the fields while a master or an overseer stood by, ready to crack his whip.

Then, one morning, something inside him roared to life. When Covey grabbed him for another beating, Frederick fought back. He didn't dare hit a white man—he could be hanged for that—but he wouldn't let Covey hit him either.

For two hours, the two wrestled. Covey tried to knock Frederick down; the boy tripped him. Covey reached for a stick in the barnyard; Frederick tossed him into a pile of cow droppings. At last, the worn-out white man gave up. He never tried to beat Frederick again.

"I was a changed being after that fight," Frederick later wrote. "I was *nothing* before; *I was a man* now."

BACK TO BALTIMORE

Frederick was sent to work on another farm. There he led four friends in making plans to escape. Someone told the master. Frederick was thrown in jail. He was afraid he would be hanged or sold to a new owner far down south, where escape was nearly impossible. Luckily, Thomas Auld decided to send his troublemaking slave back to Baltimore instead.

Frederick went to work for a shipbuilder. He was allowed to live on his own, but he still had to give part of each week's pay to his Baltimore master, Hugh Auld. He also had to pay for his own room, meals, clothes, and tools. It took long, hard work to have just a little money left over, but he was glad to do it. Working for himself made him feel one step closer to freedom.

Many black people who were already free lived in Baltimore. Some had been

Frederick worked in a Baltimore shipyard as a caulker, filling the seams of ships with a waterproof material so they wouldn't leak. Each week, he turned over most of the money he made to his master.

set free by masters who no longer needed them, while others had saved enough money to buy their freedom. One young free woman, Anna Murray, took a special liking to Frederick. Anna worked as a housekeeper for one of Baltimore's rich white families. She was gentle and warmhearted. She and Frederick fell in love. They decided to get married. Then something happened to change their plans.

ESCAPE!

In August 1838, Frederick and Hugh Auld argued. The young man was one day late making his weekly payment to his master. Hugh angrily reminded him that he was still a slave. He ordered Frederick to move back into the Aulds' house, where he could keep an eye on him. Even worse, he told Frederick that from now on he had to turn over all the money he earned.

The time had come. Frederick planned his escape. This time, he *had* to make it. If he failed, he'd be sold down south for sure.

On September 3, Frederick rode to the

Anna Douglass, Frederick's first wife. Some stories say that she sold her featherbed to raise money for his escape.

Thousands of slaves escaped to freedom in the North each year. Many others were caught and beaten or sold to slave traders far down south.

railroad station and jumped on a train just as it started moving. He was disguised as a sailor, in a red shirt and sailor's cap. In his pocket were free seaman's papers borrowed from a friend— all free blacks had to carry papers proving they weren't slaves. Scared but trying hard not to show it, he showed the papers to the conductor. Then he settled back for the long ride north.

Once, Frederick looked out the window straight at a white captain he'd worked for. The man didn't see him, and the train moved on. Later, another white man stared at him a long time, but finally looked away. "The heart of no fox or deer, with hungry hounds on his trail, … could have beaten more … noisily than did mine," he later wrote.

At last, by train and steamboat, Frederick reached New York, a Free State. "My chains were broken," he wrote, "I WAS A FREEMAN."

A NEW LIFE

New York was a Free State, but it was still a dangerous place for runaways. Slave owners sent slave catchers to New York to find runaways and bring them home. The state also had abolitionists who helped escaped slaves get farther north, where it was safer. One abolitionist helped Frederick send for Anna. The two were married. Then they headed north for Massachusetts.

Frederick and Anna settled in New Bedford. This growing city was home to many escaped slaves. When they came north, slaves changed their names to make it harder for their owners to find them. Frederick's mother had named him Frederick Augustus Washington Bailey. Now he chose a new last name—Douglass.

For the next three years, Frederick Douglass swept chimneys, sawed wood, and shoveled coal. He and Anna had two children, Rosetta and Lewis. The Douglasses were poor, but Frederick worked hard to take care of his family. He was free and proud to be his own master.

In 1838, Frederick and Anna Douglass settled in the busy shipbuilding city of New Bedford, Massachusetts.

FREEDOM'S BATTLE

In 1841, Frederick took a break from work to travel to a big meeting of abolitionists. One of the speakers would be William Lloyd Garrison, a famous abolitionist leader. Every week, Frederick read Garrison's newspaper, the *Liberator*. He loved the paper because it criticized slave

Frederick Douglass admired abolitionist leader William Lloyd Garrison and his newspaper, the Liberator. *After Frederick's first speech at an abolitionist meeting, Garrison was so impressed that he cried out, "Should such a man be held a slave?" The whole audience answered by shouting, "No! No! No!"*

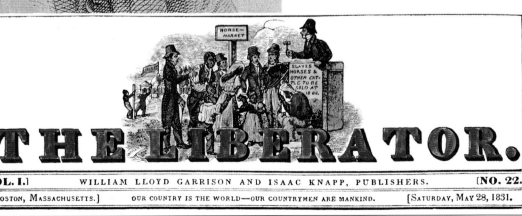

THE LIBERATOR.

VOL. I.]   WILLIAM LLOYD GARRISON AND ISAAC KNAPP, PUBLISHERS.   [NO. 22.

BOSTON, MASSACHUSETTS.]   OUR COUNTRY IS THE WORLD—OUR COUNTRYMEN ARE MANKIND.   [SATURDAY, MAY 28, 1831.

owners and demanded that all slaves be set free.

At the abolitionist meeting, someone asked Frederick to say a few words to the crowd. The young man was surprised . . . and scared. Shaking, he stood before hundreds of men and women. At first, he could hardly talk. After a few minutes, his voice grew stronger and stronger. Then a thrill ran through the crowd as the proud-looking man with the mighty voice told the story of his life as a slave.

When Frederick finished, abolitionist leaders, including his hero Garrison, rushed to shake his hand. They asked the exciting young speaker to join them in the fight against slavery. Frederick agreed. With "my whole heart . . . " he wrote, "I . . . went forth to the battle."

SPEAKING OUT

Frederick traveled across the North for four years, giving speeches in churches, parks, and meeting halls. White abolitionists often traveled with him, sharing the stage . . . and the rotten eggs thrown by listeners who hated abolition. But Frederick had a story no white person could tell—the "inside" story of a life in slavery. And he told that story in a way no one else could.

Frederick Douglass was over six feet tall, with broad shoulders and dark, fiery eyes. His voice was as deep and rich as organ music. His words were simple but powerful. Many people called him the greatest speaker alive. When he spoke, many who were against abolition changed their minds and turned against slavery instead.

Even in the Free States, black people were not allowed in "whites-only" hotels, restaurants, and train cars.

Frederick spoke about prejudice, too. Often he could not get a hotel room or a seat in a restaurant just because of the color of his skin. On steamboats, black people had to sleep out on the open decks. On trains, they were only allowed in the dirty, uncomfortable "colored" car. Frederick told about the time he refused to leave his seat in a "whites-only" car. It took six men to throw him off the train, and he brought the seat with him.

FAR FROM HOME

"He's never been a slave," many northerners began to say. Frederick spoke so beautifully that people believed he must have grown up in the North, with a good education. He had to prove them wrong. He would write a book about his life. For the first time, he would tell his real name and where he came from—even though that could make it easy for his old master to find him.

Narrative of the Life of Frederick Douglass, an American Slave came out in June 1845. The book was a great success. It made thousands of new friends for abolition. It also put Frederick's freedom in danger.

In four years of speaking, Frederick had only been home a few weeks at a time. He and Anna now had four children—Rosetta, Lewis, Frederick Jr., and Charles. Frederick missed them all. But he was not safe at home . . . or anywhere else in America.

Frederick sailed for Europe. He traveled through England, Ireland, and Scotland. He spoke to large audiences, asking for their help in the fight against American slavery. He was happy in Europe,

"I want the slaveholder surrounded, as by a wall of anti-slavery fire," Frederick told audiences in England. "I want him to feel . . . that the voice of the world is against him."

Anna and Frederick's sons: Lewis, Frederick Jr., and Charles Douglass

where blacks and whites were treated the same way. But he knew his work at home was not finished.

In 1847, Frederick returned to America. In his hands were papers proving that at last he was really free. Friends in England had bought his freedom from Thomas Auld for about $700. Those same friends had also given Frederick enough money to make another dream come true. He planned to buy a printing press. He would start a new newspaper, one published by a black man for all the black people.

Daughter Rosetta Douglass

THE GREAT BATTLE

The first issue of the *North Star* rolled off the printing press in December 1847. Frederick's newspaper would keep on rolling for the next sixteen years.

The *North Star* told stories about escaping slaves and reported on abolitionist meetings. It printed stories and poems by black writers. It told about blacks who had worked hard for success. Frederick also used his paper to speak out for women, who were fighting for equal rights with men.

As publisher of a successful newspaper, Frederick Douglass became the true leader of his people. His paper was a powerful voice for freedom. His success proved that blacks could reach any goal they set.

RUNNING THE "RAILROAD"

A soft knocking called Frederick to the door. "Who's there?" he asked. "A friend with friends." Hearing the password, Frederick quickly opened the door and let the tired, dusty travelers in.

Frederick and his family had moved to

In this painting, called The Underground Railroad, *weary slaves reach a busy "station" along the secret route to freedom.*

Rochester, New York, a few miles south of Canada. He was busy with the newspaper and with traveling and speaking, but he and Anna also had other important work. They were conductors on the Underground Railroad.

The Underground Railroad was a secret band of abolitionists set up across the country to help runaway slaves. Each helper was a "conductor." Each house was a "station." Conductors gave runaways food, clothes, and a bed, then helped them make it safely to the next station.

Many nights, Frederick and Anna heard that knock on the door and knew another frightened runaway needed a friend. Over the years, they helped thousands of slaves cross to freedom in Canada.

JOHN BROWN'S RAID

In the 1850s, more runaways than ever tried to make their way out of America. New laws had been passed giving slave owners more and more power.

One law said the government had to help slave owners hunt down runaways and bring them home. Other laws allowed slavery in areas of the West that had always been free.

Frederick and many other people began to lose hope that peaceful work would ever end slavery. One abolitionist, John Brown, tried to talk Frederick into helping him lead an army of slaves in an attack on a government weapons factory in Harper's Ferry, Virginia. Frederick said no. He was sure the plan would fail. It did, and Brown and his men were hanged.

In this painting, called The Last Moments of John Brown, *the famous abolitionist pauses on the way to his hanging.*

Suddenly Frederick was accused of helping plan the attack. With government marshals on his tail, he escaped to Canada.

A few months later, he returned. The flurry over John Brown had passed. A new excitement was sweeping the country. Elections were near, and one man running for president stood under a banner promising NO MORE SLAVE STATES.

"Into this contest I threw myself," Frederick wrote. With all his might, he worked for the election of Abraham Lincoln.

THE CIVIL WAR

Abraham Lincoln became president in 1861. Southerners were afraid he would end slavery. They decided to break away and form their own country. America

President Abraham Lincoln visits with officers of the Union army during the Civil War. Frederick called the president "an honest man—one whom I could love, honor, and trust."

divided into North and South—the Union and the Confederacy. When Confederate troops attacked a government fort, Lincoln asked Northerners to form a Union army to defeat them. The Civil War had begun.

To abolitionists, the Civil War was a war against slavery. To Lincoln, it was a war to save the Union—to make the North and the South one country again. Lincoln hated slavery, but he believed Northerners would not fight a war just to free the slaves.

Frederick set out to change his mind. In hundreds of fiery speeches, he told Northerners they would never defeat the South without the help of free black men. He demanded that Lincoln free all slaves and let blacks fight for the Union.

On January 1, 1863, Abraham Lincoln signed the Emancipation Proclamation. That order did not completely end slavery—blacks in Southern states that had not joined the Confederacy remained slaves—but it did free the slaves in the states at war with the Union. It also allowed blacks to join the army.

Frederick waited with friends for news of the proclamation's signing. When word came, he wrote, there was "joy and gladness . . . shouts of praise . . . sobs and tears."

THE BATTLES END

Two of the first black men to sign up for the army were Frederick's sons Lewis and Charles. Frederick worked hard, writing and speaking, to convince other blacks to join the fight. "This is your hour and mine," he told them. "The iron

Soldiers say good-bye to their families and head for battle in the Civil War. Brave fighting by two hundred thousand black volunteers helped the Union army win the war.

gate of our prison stands half open." To win freedom for all their people, blacks must do their part for the Union.

Nearly two hundred thousand black men joined the Union army. They fought bravely and helped the North win many battles. But they weren't treated fairly. In 1863, Frederick took the problem to President Lincoln.

Black soldiers got less pay than whites, he told the president, and they were never rewarded for bravery. Worst of all, blacks captured by Confederate soldiers often were murdered or sold into slavery. Lincoln listened carefully. He promised to help. A few days later, he ordered strong punishment for the murder or sale of black prisoners. In time, black soldiers got equal pay, and a few received medals for bravery.

By 1865, after four years of war, it was clear the North was winning. The Civil War ended on April 9. A few months later, the Thirteenth Amendment to the United States Constitution ended slavery forever.

CROWNING HONORS

Slavery had ended, but there were battles still to fight. The former slaves had no rights and no power. Frederick pushed for laws making blacks American citizens. Then he led the fight for one of a citizen's most important powers. In 1870 his work was rewarded. The Fifteenth Amendment to the Constitution gave African American men the right to vote.

To the Capital

America's capital, Washington, D.C., was the place for a citizen so interested in laws and government. There Frederick published a newspaper called the *New National Era*. For a while, he was also president of a bank for one-time slaves.

Frederick still traveled and spoke. Many of his speeches were about government. His powerful words helped elect presidents who he believed would protect the rights of African Americans. Frederick served three of these presidents in important government posts. Such honors had never before been given to an African American. To Frederick, the honors were for his people, too.

In his later years, Frederick Douglass's fiery looks and powerful voice earned him the nickname "the black lion." When people complained that the "lion" roared too loud, Frederick answered that there can be no freedom without "an earnest struggle . . . no . . . rain without thunder and lightning."

Frederick named his grand home in Washington, D.C. "Cedar Hill," because the lands surrounding it were filled with cedar trees. He enjoyed getting up at five each morning to walk the grounds.

MANY CHANGES

Frederick turned sixty in 1878. To celebrate, he bought a grand new house. The slave boy who had slept in Old Master's kitchen closet was now master of twenty rooms on a hill high above the nation's capital.

He was still tall and strong, with fiery eyes and flowing white hair. But Anna was sickly. She had long spells of weakness. In 1882, she died.

Frederick felt lost. He and Anna hadn't always been happy—his work came first, and she couldn't share in that. Anna never learned to read, and she felt uncomfortable around his educated friends. But for forty-four years, she had stood by him. The grand house seemed empty without her.

In time, a new love filled the emptiness. Frederick married Helen Pitts, a

Frederick married his second wife, Helen Pitts, in 1844.

small, dark-haired woman active in the fight for women's rights. People were shocked. Helen was white. But Frederick ignored the prejudice. He and Helen were in love, and it was no one's business, he wrote, if his wife was "the complexion [color] of my father rather than that of my mother."

The Douglasses lived in Haiti for two years. Frederick was proud to serve as the United States' first African American minister to another country, especially since Haiti was the first free black country in the West. They returned home in 1891. Frederick was seventy-three years old, famous, respected, rich . . . and tired.

A FINAL BATTLE

Frederick added a few chapters to a third book about his life. Then he put down his pen like a weary traveler "at the desired end of a long journey." But the journey wasn't ended yet.

In the years since the Civil War, the old forces of hatred and prejudice had grown strong again. Freed slaves in the South were forced to work for almost no pay. New laws made it impossible for them to buy land or get an education. Unfair election laws kept them from voting. African Americans who stood up for their rights were beaten or lynched— hanged, shot, or even burned to death by angry mobs.

Living in Washington, in his fine home, Frederick had lost sight of his people's suffering. A young woman named Ida B. Wells opened his eyes. Ida wrote and spoke about the terrible conditions in the South. She asked Frederick to give his great voice to the fight. Then the fire that had burned in him for the battle against slavery blazed again.

In articles and speeches, Frederick thundered down on the lynch mobs. He demanded the end of prejudice and the beginnings of true freedom.

On February 20, 1895, Frederick spoke at a women's rights meeting. That night, at home, he died of a heart attack. He was seventy-seven years old.

He would not see the end of his last great battle, but his words would light the way for leaders to come. For African Americans—for all Americans—Frederick Douglass was a bright star shining with the promise of equality and freedom for all people.

For many years after the Civil War, lynch mobs terrorized African Americans in the South.

Glossary

abolition: The ending of slavery. *Abolish* means to put an end to. Abolitionists were people who worked to end slavery.

amendment: A new ruling added to the U.S. Constitution.

Confederacy/Confederate: The Southern forces in the Civil War.

Emancipation Proclamation: The order that freed the slaves in the Confederacy. *Emancipation* means setting free. A proclamation is a government order.

Free States: States in the North where, by 1804, slavery had been abolished.

lynch: To kill by a mob.

master: A man who owned slaves.

mistress: A woman who owned slaves.

plantation: A very large farm.

prejudice: Hating a group of people because of their color or for some other unfair reason.

slavery: When one person owns another.

Underground Railroad: A secret group of abolitionists who helped runaway slaves.

Union: The Northern forces in the Civil War.

To Learn More About Frederick Douglass

Your school library or local library probably has many good books about Frederick Douglass and his times. Here are some especially good ones:

Books on Frederick Douglass:

A Picture Book of Frederick Douglass by David A. Adler, published by Holiday House, 1993.

Frederick Douglass by Melissa Banta, published by Chelsea Juniors, 1993.

Frederick Douglass Fights for Freedom by Margaret Davidson, published by Scholastic, 1989.

Young Frederick Douglass: The Slave Who Learned to Read by Linda W. Girard, published by Albert Whitman, 1994.

Books on African American leaders and on slavery:

The Underground Railroad by Raymond Bial, published by Houghton Mifflin, 1995.

Go Free or Die: A Story about Harriet Tubman by Jeri Ferris, published by Carolrhoda, 1988.

Walking the Road to Freedom: A Story about Sojourner Truth by Jeri Ferris, published by Carolrhoda, 1988.

Afro-Bets Book of Black Heroes from A to Z: An Introduction to Important Black Achievers for Young Readers by Wade Hudson and Valerie Wilson Wesley, published by Just Us Books, 1988.

Also look for these videotapes:

The House of Dies Drear, Wonderworks Series, Public Media [a story of the Underground Railroad].

Frederick Douglass: When the Lion Wrote History, Greater Washington Educational Telecommunications Association, coproduced by Roja Productions and WETA-TV, Washington, D.C., 1994.

If you ever travel to Washington, D.C., you'll want to visit the Frederick Douglass National Historic Site. Here Douglass's home, Cedar Hill, has been turned into a museum. You can see a film about his life, plus many of his treasured belongings. The phone number is 202-426-5960.

Index

Page numbers for illustrations are in boldface

ABOUT THE AUTHOR

"When I read accounts by people who heard Frederick Douglass speak, it makes me sad that in those days there were no movie cameras or tape recorders. We may not be able to witness his stirring speeches, but we are lucky that this daring leader left us his life story, in words that still inspire us today."

Virginia Schomp is a freelance writer whose books for young readers include *The Bottlenose Dolphin; The Ancient Greeks; Russia: New Freedoms, New Challenges;* and *New York: Crown of Empire.* She lives in Monticello, New York, with her husband, Richard, and their son, Chip.